THE STORY OF

BOEING®

STEVEN FERRY

SMART APPLE MEDIA MANKATO MINNESOTA

Published by Smart Apple Media
123 South Broad Street, Mankato, Minnesota 56001

Copyright © 2000 Smart Apple Media.
International copyrights reserved in all countries.
No part of this book may be reproduced in any form without written
permission from the publisher.

Produced by The Creative Spark, San Juan Capistrano, CA
    Editor: Elizabeth Sirimarco
    Designer: Mary Francis-DeMarois
    Art Direction: Robert Court
    Page Layout: Jo Maurine Wheeler

Photo credits: Corbis/National Aviation Museum 4; Corbis Bettman 6, 18;
Corbis/Museum of Flight 8, 10, 11, 16, 20; Corbis/Museum of History and
Industry 9; Corbis/George Halt 12, 13; Corbis/Museum of Flight 14; Corbis/
Seattle Post/Intelligencer/Museum of History and Industry 17; Corbis/Roger
Wood; Corbis/Neil Rabinowitz 24; Archive Photos 25, 29; Aero Graphics, Inc./
©Corbis; Earl Young/Archive Photos 28; Corbis/James L. Amos 30;
Courtesy of The Boeing Company 33, 37, 39, 40; Corbis/Leif Skoogfors
34; Corbis 35.

Library of Congress Cataloging-in-Publication Data

Ferry, Steven, 1953–
     The story of Boeing / by Steven Ferry.
     p. cm. — (Spirit of success)
     Includes index.
     SUMMARY: Describes the origins and growth of the highly successful aircraft
manufacturer, Boeing, from the first airplane built by Bill Boeing in 1917 to
the satellites and stealth airplane it is making at the end of the 20th century.
     ISBN 1-58340-000-1 (alk. paper)
     1. Boeing Company—History—Juvenile literature. 2. Aircraft industry—
United States—History—Juvenile literature. 3. Conglomerate corporations—
United States—History—Juvenile literature. [1. Boeing Company—History.
2. Aircraft industry—History.] I. Title. II. Series.
     HD9711.U63 B6328 1999
     338.7′62913334′0973—dc 21
                                                                98-47572

First edition

9   8   7   6   5   4   3   2   1

Table of Contents

From Hobby to Big Business   4

Persistence, Courage, and Hard Work   14

The Jet Age   22

The American Military in Flight   26

Making Missiles, Invading Space   30

Important Moments   42

Glossary   44

Index   46

Further Information   48

From Hobby to Big Business

On July 4, 1914, Bill Boeing, a 33-year-old business-man, flew on an airplane for the first time. There were no passenger seats then. He and a friend, Conrad Westervelt, sat on the front edge of the plane's wing and held on tight. The first airplane flight had taken place about a decade earlier when, in 1903, the Wright brothers flew for just 12 seconds. By the time Boeing had his first chance to fly, airplanes could travel all the way across the North American continent, but it still took seven days to accomplish the feat—with many stops to refuel.

While many pioneers helped human beings learn to fly, the business sense of Bill Boeing helped to make **aviation** more than a dangerous and exciting pastime. Boeing and Westervelt first decided to build a plane for fun, but they soon realized that airplanes could be much more than a hobby. They knew airplanes could provide faster transportation than trains, boats, horses—or even the new "horseless carriages" (automobiles) that had appeared 20 years earlier. Boeing and Westervelt decided to manufacture airplanes and founded the B&W Company.

It was not long before America became involved in World War I. Westervelt decided to join the Navy, while Boeing built B&W's first airplane, made of wood and canvas, with the help of an engineer. The company improved the design of its first airplane and built another in 1917. The new design was far superior, and the U.S. Navy purchased 50 of them. Bill Boeing changed the name of the company to the Boeing Airplane Company. From that time forward, Boeing® has been a major supplier to the U.S. military.

The war ended in 1918, and the military no longer needed new airplanes. Almost all U.S. airplane manufacturers went out of business. To keep his company alive, Bill Boeing decided to find something else to manufacture. The company had crafted airplanes from wood, and many of its employees were skilled woodworkers. Boeing and his

aviation

The operation of aircraft.

5

Bill Boeing, who came from Seattle, Washington, was a successful businessman in the lumber industry. From the first time he saw an airplane fly until he retired from his company in 1934, Boeing thought of new ways that aviation might improve transportation in the United States—and around the world.

team tried to produce everything from beds to hat racks—almost anything they could craft from wood. Unfortunately, the products did not sell, and the company was forced to **lay off** many of its 337 employees.

Bill Boeing realized that if he wanted to succeed, his company should focus on what it did best. It needed to produce top-quality airplanes and then find a way to sell more of them. Boeing and his team began to think of new ways to use airplanes. One idea was to make "flying boats"—**seaplanes** that could deliver mail more quickly between Seattle and Vancouver. It was a good idea, and the U.S. Postal Service placed an order with Boeing. Unfortunately, it was not enough to help the company's financial situation. By 1920, the Boeing Airplane Company was $300,000 in debt—a huge sum at the time. Bill Boeing used profits from his successful lumber business to support his airplane company. At one point, he even tried to sell his airplane business, but no one wanted to buy it.

Then the U.S. Army began to recognize the value an air force could provide to its military forces. Army officials asked airplane manufacturers to bid on the production of 200 new airplanes. Six other aviation companies competed for the contract, but Boeing won the job. Bill Boeing said his company could produce the planes for $1.4 million—almost $1 million less than its competitors. Unfortunately, it was not enough to pay for the planes, and the company continued to lose money. Nonetheless, Boeing's reputation for high-quality airplanes at reasonable prices was born.

lay off

To dismiss employees not because they are doing a poor job but because the company needs to save money.

seaplanes

Airplanes with floats instead of wheels so they can take off and land on water.

The framework of Boeing and Westervelt's first plane, which they called the Sport Trainer.

In 1926, the U.S. Congress passed the Air Commerce Act. It established rules and routes for air travel in America, opening the skies to the possibility of **civilian** air travel. Previously, only stunt pilots and the military had seen the value of airplanes. Boeing immediately recognized a new market for its product. It formed the Boeing Air Transport Company to fly both people and mail from Chicago to San Francisco for the U.S. Postal Service. On July 2, 1927, its first flight took place with one passenger on board, a 20-year-old reporter named Jane Eads. The flight of the Boeing Model 40 took 23 hours and marked the beginning of air travel for American civilians.

The Boeing Model 40 used an engine designed by a company called Pratt & Whitney. Unlike those found in other airplanes, this engine used air to cool itself instead of water, so Boeing's airplanes did not need to carry a water supply. Competitors' planes could only carry water and mail, while Boeing planes had enough room to carry two

civilian

Referring to a country's citizens, as opposed to its military.

A factory at the Boeing facility in 1922.

passengers in addition to the mail. Soon the U.S. Postal Service ordered 25 more Boeing Model 40s. By 1928, Boeing reported profits of $9 million.

In 1929, Boeing completed a **merger** with Pratt & Whitney and other aviation companies to form United Aircraft and Transport (UA&T). The new company not only made its own airplanes, but operated a large, new airline as well. UA&T wanted to build larger, more comfortable planes that would attract people to travel by air. Soon it introduced an airplane with 12 reclining seats, ventilation and heating,

The U.S. Postal Service used the Boeing Model 40 on many different mail routes. When a crew stopped to refuel on a flight from Texas to Mexico City, a team of oxen transported fuel to the mail plane.

Passengers board the first all-metal airplane, the Boeing 247.

a soundproof **fuselage,** a lavatory, reading lights, and large windows. For the first time, passengers could even eat meals, served by flight attendants, on a flight.

Boeing's innovations continued. In 1933, it built the first all-metal airplane, the Boeing 247. This new craft was capable of speeds up to 200 miles (320 kilometers) per hour. It could cross the United States, making seven stops, in only 20 hours.

Bill Boeing decided it was time to retire. After years of struggle, his company had finally found success. The Boeing Airplane Company, and later UA&T, had built half the airplanes made for civilian travel, half those purchased by the U.S. Navy, and almost one-third of those used by the U.S. Air Corps.

Up and Away

    Four factors play a role in an airplane's ability to fly: lift, weight (gravity), thrust, and drag. Drag is the air's resistance to the airplane's forward motion, and thrust is the power produced by the airplane's engine to counteract that resistance.

    Lift is the upward push of an airplane that compensates for gravity. Scientific principles explain how lift works. Sir Isaac Newton, an English scientist who lived in the 17th century, said that for every action, there must be an opposite and equal reaction. It was his third law of motion.

    Without lift, the engine's thrust would cause the heavy airplane to race along the runway, but it would never take off. The wings on an airplane cause lift because as an airplane moves, its wings push air downward. According to Newton's law, an opposite action (a reaction) must occur. Thus, air pushes the bottom surface of the wing and the airplane upward, accounting for about 30 percent of an airplane's lift.

The Bernoulli effect explains the other 70 percent of an airplane's lift. Daniel Bernoulli was a Swiss scientist who lived in the 18th century. Bernoulli's law says that an increase in velocity (speed) reduces drag. Drag is the resistance of the air against the fast-moving airplane.

As air rushes past an airplane's wing, it must travel farther over the curved upper surface of the wing than under the flatter lower surface. Thus, the air moves more quickly over the top of the wing than the bottom. According to Bernoulli's law, the faster-moving air exerts less downward pressure (drag) on the wing, pushing the wing and the airplane upward.

Persistence, Courage, and Hard Work

Things were looking up for the company when Bill Boeing retired in 1933. Unfortunately, a major setback occurred the following year. The Great Depression had left many people without jobs or a means to support their families. Americans began to think that big businesses and **monopolies** were making too much money. In 1935, the U.S. government passed a law stating that airplane manufacturers and airlines could not be part of a single company. UA&T split into five smaller companies: United Airlines, United Airlines Transport (today known as UTC), the engine manufacturer Pratt & Whitney, and the propeller manufacturer Hamilton Steel. Boeing® continued to manufacture airplanes.

At the same time, despite Boeing's past success, competitors had begun to make superior airplanes. A company called Douglas produced the DC-2, an aluminum airplane that was less expensive than Boeing's 247 and could cross the United States in just 12 hours. Lockheed's new Electra was also a more efficient airplane, and soon the Boeing 247 slipped into third place.

Boeing began to concentrate on making larger airplanes. The Boeing 314 seaplane could carry 74 passengers nonstop for 4,275 miles (6,840 kilometers) at 150 miles (240 kilometers) per hour. President Franklin D. Roosevelt, the first president to fly, traveled on one of these luxurious 314 "Clippers" in January 1943.

Boeing also built the B-17 Bomber, which became famous during World War II as the Flying Fortress. The B-17 was much better than similar models made by other manufacturers, and the Air Corps ordered 14 of them.

Next, Boeing added the Stratocruiser to its fleet of large airplanes. It had four engines and could cruise in the **stratosphere.** A plane that can fly so high avoids the bad weather that makes passengers airsick. This feature made it an excellent model for civilian airlines, whose passengers often experienced motion sickness.

monopolies

The ownership and control of products or industries by single companies.

stratosphere

The upper portion of the atmosphere, which extends from approximately seven miles (11 kilometers) to about 31 miles (50 kilometers) above the Earth. Temperature changes little in the stratosphere, and clouds are rare.

The higher an airplane can fly, the faster it can go because the air is thinner and therefore creates less resistance. Once Boeing designed a plane that could fly high enough to avoid bad weather and reach high speeds, it had another problem to tackle. The air at such high altitudes is so thin that people cannot breathe. Boeing invented the first pressurized cabin to solve this problem. It provided the same amount of air in the cabin as there was on the ground. Here Boeing employees check a cabin for possible leaks in a pressurized cabin.

Boeing converted 56 of its Stratocruisers into civilian airplanes that could carry 72 to 100 passengers. Unfortunately, the engines were unreliable, and Boeing lost $15 million on the project.

Once again, it was military orders that saved Boeing from **bankruptcy.** During World War II, the United States spent $185 billion on weapons; it spent $46 billion of this sum on airplanes. American companies built more than 300,000 airplanes between 1939 and 1945.

Boeing's female employees learn metal-working skills during World War II.

Lt. General James Doolittle after his first flight on a Boeing B-29 Superfortress. "It's a fine airplane and handles nicely," said Doolittle. B-29s were sturdy—one even managed to land while it was on fire from nose to tail, riddled with 2,000 bullet holes.

Making airplanes during a war is not the same as during peacetime. Because many men joined the military, women made up half the Boeing work force. Boeing was one of the most important airplane manufacturers. Concerned that the Japanese would try to bomb the company's plant, the U.S. government decided to hide it using camouflage. It constructed imaginary towns with houses, roads, cars, and trees and placed them on top of all Boeing facilities.

Inside this imaginary town, Boeing produced more than 12,000 B-17s, averaging 15 each day at peak production. Boeing also built 2,700 of the giant B-29 Superfortresses. Although B-29s made up only 17 percent of the U.S. bomber force during the war, they dropped 46 percent of the bombs on Germany and 99 percent on Japan. These massive airplanes also shot down 67 percent of the German fighters.

As in the past, when the war ended, demand for airplanes declined—and so did the number of employees at Boeing. During World War II, Boeing employed approximately 51,000 people. Once the war was over, only 7,500 employees remained.

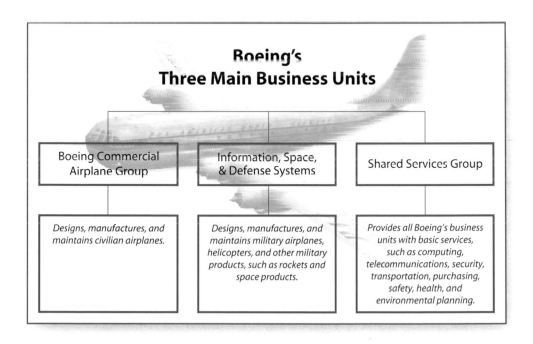

Boeing's Three Main Business Units

Boeing Commercial Airplane Group	Information, Space, & Defense Systems	Shared Services Group
Designs, manufactures, and maintains civilian airplanes.	*Designs, manufactures, and maintains military airplanes, helicopters, and other military products, such as rockets and space products.*	*Provides all Boeing's business units with basic services, such as computing, telecommunications, security, transportation, purchasing, safety, health, and environmental planning.*

Boeing decided to turn its attention to **jet** technology. Even at the end of the war, the threat of future conflicts existed. Although the United States and the Soviet Union had once been allies, they now fought the "Cold War." No actual battles were fought, but both nations were ready to fight back in the event that the other attacked.

Boeing designed and built 2,100 B-47s, the first jet bomber and the forerunner of modern civilian jets. They were built to deliver nuclear bombs in the event of a war against the Soviet Union. Many say it was the existence of such deadly weapons and the means to deliver them that prevented a war.

A Boeing B-52 bomber flies above the clouds in 1957.

In 1951, Boeing followed the B-47 with the B-52 Stratofortress bomber, an eight-engine airplane that remains in service today. The Stratofortress could fly at an amazing 600 miles (960 kilometers) per hour for 7,000 miles (11,200 kilometers). It could carry more than 50,000 pounds (22,780 kilograms) and launch **cruise missiles.**

Boeing's history illustrates the fact that there is a greater demand for airplanes at certain times than others. In each period in which customers purchased fewer airplanes, from 1918 through the 1970s, Boeing tried and failed to **diversify** into other product markets.

The willingness to try something new has always led Boeing to take big risks. In 1969, Boeing completed production of a Jumbo Jet with 500 seats, the 747® model. Producing this jet was a gamble that almost left the company bankrupt. Airlines found they could not fill enough seats on the 747 and canceled their orders for the giant jet. Boeing went 17 months without selling a single civilian jetliner during 1969 and 1970.

Boeing took its usual course of action for tough times. It laid off 89,000 of its 142,000 employees between 1969 and 1971. Success would follow, however. Over the next two decades, Boeing sold more than 1,000 of the 747 model, accounting for 70 percent of its profits.

cruise missiles

Guided missiles that fly low, using radar to avoid hitting anything on the way to their target.

diversify

To increase the variety of products a company sells or produces.

The Jet Age

I n 1953, a British company named De Havilland
introduced the first jet for civilian travel, the Comet.
In just 13 months, Boeing® developed the Dash 80
to compete against it. The company had a ready-to-fly
Dash 80, later known as the Boeing 707®, by May 1954.
Meanwhile, the Comet was withdrawn after two of them
had crashed, killing everyone on board. Boeing's engineers

believed **metal fatigue** created this problem and designed the Dash 80 to avoid it. The hard work paid off when the airline PanAm ordered 20 Dash 80s in October 1955. The 707's first transatlantic flight, from New York to Brussels, took place three years later.

Boeing kept improving its jets. In 1967, Boeing released the 737®, which has since become the best-selling airliner in aviation history. In January 1970, Boeing introduced its 747® Jumbo Jet to the public. The first flight departed for London from Washington, D.C. Unfortunately, an engine overheated before the pilot could take off, but PanAm officials had the foresight to prepare for an emergency. Another 747 was waiting in a hanger, and PanAm staff transferred the passengers to the other plane. The first transatlantic flight of the 747 went forward with little delay. Today the 747 is produced in the world's largest factory, which covers 63 acres (25.5 hectares) in Everett, Washington. The airplane has 4.5 million parts, is almost the length of a football field, and rises six stories high at the tail.

Boeing released its latest airliner, the 777®, in April 1994. It cost $5.5 billion to develop. Each engine produces 80,000 pounds of thrust, which is the weight a jet engine can push.

In 1997, Boeing merged with one-time competitor McDonnell Douglas, becoming the world's largest **aerospace** company. This added a few more commercial airliners to its **inventory.** Boeing has built more than 12,000 jet airliners since the first order of 707s in 1955, and more than 9,000 of these are still flying.

metal fatigue

When metal breaks apart from repeated stress.

aerospace

All the companies that create technology and products to enable travel in the Earth's atmosphere and into space.

inventory

The list of products produced by a company or products that it currently has in stock.

Boeing introduced the latest 747 model, the series 400, in 1988. About 60 percent of the world's airliners are Boeing jets, and Boeing makes 50 new civilian jets each month. In 1990, Boeing jets carried 675 million passengers, or 12 percent of the world's total population.

Air Force One

Boeing has manufactured the U.S. president's personal airplane since 1943 when President Roosevelt first flew on the 314 Clipper. Today Air Force One is a Boeing 747, modified in 1990. This airplane replaced the Boeing 707, used by past presidents for nearly 30 years.

The "Flying Oval Office" has 4,000 square feet (1,220 square meters) of floor space, with a conference/dining room, quarters for the president and his family, and an office area for senior staff members.

Another office can be converted into a medical facility, and there are work and rest areas for the president's staff, the media, and the crew. Two kitchens can feed up to 100 people. Air Force One has 238 miles (380 kilometers) of electrical wiring—twice the normal amount found in a 747. It also boasts 85 telephones and communications radios, allowing the passengers and crew to stay in touch with the rest of the world at all times.

The American Military in Flight

While Boeing® has been supplying the world's commercial airlines with a wide selection of airplanes, it has also continued to be the major supplier of airplanes for the U.S. armed forces. The company continued its line of large bombers with the B-1 in 1984 and has built 100 of them for the U.S. Air Force. The B-2 **stealth** bomber is the world's most advanced aircraft and can fly direct to anywhere in the world from North America. It is the first of the stealth aircraft, built so that an enemy cannot detect it with **radar.**

Boeing's fighter jets are equally advanced. By swinging its engines from a vertical to a horizontal position, the Harrier jump jet can actually "morph" from a type of helicopter into a jet airplane. This feature allows it to take off from and land in small spaces. Boeing teamed up with a company called British Aerospace to design and build the Harrier jump jet. The F-15 Eagle is the most efficient fighter in the world. Since 1974, the military has used it to shoot down almost 100 airplanes. Of the 35 airplanes Iraq lost in the air during the Gulf War, 33 were shot down by F-15s.

Boeing has teamed with Lockheed Martin to develop the F-22 Raptor to replace the F-15. A raptor is a bird of prey, such as an eagle or hawk, and the F-22 is designed to rule the skies like one. It is another stealth aircraft, designed to locate and shoot an enemy before it shows up on radar.

Boeing also makes fuel tankers and transporters, continuing the company's tradition of making large airplanes. The KC-10 and KC-135A entered the Air Force fleet in 1957. In 1998, 550 of the 732 built were still flying. The military also uses the Boeing 767 for refueling and airlift missions.

The C-17 is the latest and largest transporter. During testing in 1995, it set 22 world records, primarily for how much weight it can carry and how high it can fly. The four engines each produce more than 40,000 pounds (18,150 kilograms) of thrust and can carry 169,000 pounds (76,660 kilograms) of weight.

stealth

The design of an aircraft that avoids vertical surfaces and uses special paint so that radar signals are absorbed, making the plane difficult for an enemy to spot.

radar

A device that detects radio waves to determine the location, distance, and speed of an object.

A C-17 can land on a rough 1,400-foot (472-meter) runway and can turn itself around in a space 80 yards (72 meters) wide—even with a wingspan nearly three-quarters that long. Most aircraft cannot reverse themselves on the ground and usually require a truck to push them.

Boeing has converted several of its large airplanes for special missions. In 1970, they made several Boeing 707 aircraft into AWACS (Airborne Warning and Control System), with special radar equipment on top. These airplanes are like spies in the sky, used to detect enemy aircraft from great distances. They also monitor air traffic during attack or defense situations.

Boeing modified four of its aircraft to act as airborne command offices for U.S. military officers. Generals can command their troops from these aircraft in the event that ground headquarters are destroyed.

The company expanded into the production of helicopters in 1960 when it bought the Vertol Aircraft Corporation. Vertol had just introduced the H-46 Sea Knight and the CH-47 Chinook. The Special Operation Chinook is designed for use by covert operations forces. It can travel 400 miles (640 kilometers) at low levels in five hours, day or night, regardless of the weather.

Boeing has since joined forces with other companies to make more helicopters. In 1981, it began producing the V-22 Osprey (similar to the Harrier jump jet) with Bell Helicopters, a Texas manufacturer. Once airborne, the Osprey can tilt its **rotors,** turn them into propellers, and then fly like a plane. In 1991, Boeing worked with another rival, Sikorsky, to build the RAH-66 Comanche—the most advanced helicopter in the world.

Boeing was part of the team, led by Northrop-Grumman, that built the B-2 stealth bomber.

Making Missiles, Invading Space

Missiles are an important part of the United States' defense against nuclear attack. After World War II, Boeing® developed ground-to-air pilotless aircraft (GAPA) missiles that could shoot down other aircraft. The company soon made a longer range missile called Bomarc, which the Minuteman missile replaced in the early 1970s. The Minuteman III can travel 6,000 miles (960 kilometers) at 15,000 miles (24,000 kilometers) per hour.

Boeing built a dozen different missiles for the military that can attack tanks, ships, airplanes, underground bunkers, and other missiles. Boeing also makes several **tactical missile** systems, which include the computerized machinery that fires and controls a missile. In addition, Boeing is building a space-based defense system, the National Missile Defense (NMD), that will protect the United States from **ballistic missile** attacks. It can detect and track an enemy missile in space so that ground-based missiles can shoot it down before it can do any damage.

Boeing was one of the first companies to turn travel in outer space into a reality. Its first attempt at space travel, the Dyna-Soar (which stands for "Dyna"mic and "Soar"ing), never made it past the drawing boards. Designed in 1957 as a space-craft that could also fly and land like a plane, it was 20 years ahead of the space shuttle, which does the same things today.

In 1960, Boeing began to make **rocket boosters.** More than 250 Delta launch vehicles have been produced for NASA since then. The latest, Delta IV, can transport 33,000 pounds (15,000 kilograms) to 22,000 miles (35,000 kilometers) above Earth. Rocket boosters, such as the Delta series, send the satellites used to relay telephone communications and TV signals into space. Boeing built the five Lunar Orbital Vehicles that flew around the Moon in 1966, relaying pictures of possible landing sites back to NASA and taking the first pictures of Earth. Boeing also built the first stage of the Saturn S-1C three-stage rocket that carried the spaceship *Apollo* to the moon.

missiles

Rockets with explosive weapons used to destroy a target from a distance.

tactical missile

A missile with a short range for use at the battlefront.

ballistic missile

A missile that is guided only at the time of launch and then falls freely to its target. By contrast, guided missiles are powered and steered throughout their time in the air.

rocket boosters

Rockets that help launch another craft, such as the space shuttle or a missile.

navigation

The science of directing a ship, aircraft, or spacecraft from one place to another.

Global Positioning System (GPS)

Satellites that transmit signals to earth. When signals from these satellites are received, they can pinpoint a person or object's location.

In 1971, Boeing helped General Motors build three Lunar Rover Vehicles used to drive astronauts around the moon. With a top speed of 9 miles (14 kilometers) per hour, the Rovers weren't the fastest Boeing vehicles, and they could travel only 60 miles (96 kilometers) before their batteries ran out.

Boeing also builds various parts of the space shuttle, including its main engines. The company is currently working on Highly Reusable Space Transportation (HRST). It would be very expensive to fly around the country if airlines had to throw away each airplane after only one flight, yet this is how aerospace companies have designed their spacecraft in the past. Boeing wants to change this by developing reusable rockets.

The 16-nation Space Station is the largest international project of its kind, with Brazil, Canada, 11 members of the European Union, Japan, Russia, and the United States working together to make it happen. When completed in 2003, it will be two football fields in size and will house six people. The Station will orbit 250 miles (400 kilometers) above Earth, providing a permanent laboratory for scientific research that cannot be conducted on the ground. When work first began on the Space Station, the U.S. government chose Boeing to lead the American team.

Boeing also builds satellites. It revolutionized **navigation** by building the **Global Positioning System** satellites. These can help a person pinpoint his or her location to within 100 feet (30.5 meters) by using a

Scientists from 16 nations are cooperating to build the Space Station, which will provide a laboratory for research in space.

hand-held box to communicate with the satellites. This is useful whether a person is lost or simply seeking directions from one point to another on land, in the air, or on water. Some car manufacturers have even included GPS in their latest models to help drivers find their way without a map. GPS satellites can also track the location of people or things. If hikers wear a matchbox-sized receiver, a search party can locate them with GPS should they become lost.

Another Boeing satellite, ARGOS, collects information in the Earth's upper atmosphere for use in military and environmental programs. Boeing is also working with Teledesic Corporation to create a network of several hundred satellites. Such technology will bring affordable, high-quality telephone service, as well as Internet access, to

A U.S. soldier uses a Global Positioning System device.

An Air Force Delta launch vehicle prepares to carry a satellite system into orbit.

even the most remote regions of the planet. Until recently, only people living in developed areas had access to modern communication systems. Other Boeing satellites allow schools or companies to transmit live video so that a student who lives far away can attend class or an overseas business partner can attend a meeting transmitted via satellite.

Among the most exciting of Boeing's recent projects is DarkStar, a stealth airplane that flies at 45,000 feet (14,000 meters) above battlefields for eight hours, sending information back to headquarters—all without a pilot. It first flew in 1996 and is Boeing's most advanced UAV (Unmanned Aerial Vehicle).

Today Boeing still focuses its efforts within the aerospace industry, but it has a much greater variety of customers than ever before. If demand for one Boeing product declines, others will keep the company profitable. Boeing makes more than one dozen different civilian jet airliners and even more military fighters, bombers, and tankers. It also manufactures six models of helicopters, several rockets, satellites, the space shuttle, and many different missiles. It leads the U.S. team responsible for the Space Station. All of these projects have made it an American success story.

Boeing has customers in 145 countries around the world, employees in more than 60 nations, and facilities in 27 U.S. states. In mid-1998, Boeing had 238,000 employees who sent three million e-mails each day and earned more than $6 billion in a single year.

Boeing worked with another aerospace company, Lockheed Martin, to build DarkStar.

Even with its ongoing success, Boeing has faced its share of problems. Like other aerospace companies, Boeing ran into trouble when officials learned the company had overcharged the U.S. government for millions of dollars in research and development fees. The government accused Boeing of drastically increasing the price of tools and materials used in military projects. In 1994, Boeing returned $475 million of such charges. Along with other aerospace companies, Boeing has since answered to strict spending guidelines set by the U.S. government.

strike

To stop working in an attempt to force an employer to agree to certain demands, such as an increase in pay or fewer layoffs.

Over the years, the company has continued to lay off employees when times were tough. It laid off one-third of its workers between 1990 and 1995. This upset employees so much that they decided to **strike.** In 1995, a 69-day strike cost the company $2 billion. More layoffs followed. At the end of the 1990s, many nations, such as Japan and Russia, experienced financial difficulties. Because many of Boeing's customers are outside the United States, the problems of other nations can hurt its sales. In response to declining sales of civilian aircraft, Boeing officials laid off 48,000 employees in 1998.

Despite these setbacks, Boeing has continued to expand. It purchased the defense and space units of Rockwell International in 1996. Earnings for 1997 were $45.8 billion, 70 percent of which were earned from civilian aircraft. In December 1998, NASA selected Boeing to develop a new unpiloted space vehicle, the Future X Pathfinder.

In addition to its aerospace interests, Boeing focuses its attention on the research and development of new technologies. Some Boeing scientists investigate the effects of radiation on the materials it uses in its products. Others attempt to capture the energy of the sun for use on Earth, offering human beings an unlimited supply of energy.

Since Bill Boeing first founded his airplane company, its products have changed the world of transportation. The company has revolutionized civilian air travel and helped the U.S. government remain powerful. It has given the United States the equipment it needs to assist other nations. It has helped human beings take their first steps into outer space. Whether harnessing the limitless energy of the sun or building the world's first international space station, Boeing will continue to develop exciting, new technology.

Russian scientists work on the Zarya Functional Cargo Block in Moscow. When the Space Station is complete it will be the length of a football field.

The B&W Company built its first airplane in 1916, and Bill Boeing's company has played a vital role in the aerospace industry ever since. Today's technology is so advanced, aircraft such as DarkStar don't even need a pilot.

The Drive to Carry More, Farther

Compare the capabilities of Boeing's first airplane, built in 1916, with the biggest plane it manufactured in 1999, the 747-400.

	1916	1999 (747-400)
Weight	2,800 pounds 1,270 kilograms	870,000 pounds 394,545 kilograms
Wingspan	52 feet 16 meters	213 feet 65 meters
Speed	75 miles/hour 120 kilometers/hour	500 miles/hour 800 kilometers/hour
Number of Passengers	2	416
Range*	320 miles 512 kilometers	8,380 miles 13,408 kilometers
Price	$10,000	$177 million

The distance the plane can travel without stopping.

Important Moments

1914
William Boeing and Conrad Westervelt fly for the first time and later start the B&W Company.

1916
B&W builds its first plane.

1917
B&W changes its name to the Boeing Airplane Company. The U.S. Navy buys 50 Boeing airplanes.

1927
Boeing pioneers mail and passenger air travel between Chicago and San Francisco.

1933
Boeing introduces the first all-metal airplane, the Boeing 247.

1943
Boeing introduces the B-29 Superfortress.

1951
Boeing introduces the B-52 Stratofortress.

1954
Boeing completes the first successful civilian jet, the Dash 80/Boeing 707.

1958
The first transatlantic passenger flight of a Boeing jet takes place.

1960
Boeing produces the first of its successful Delta rockets for NASA.

1966
Boeing's Lunar Orbital Vehicles fly around the moon.

1969
Boeing completes production of the first 747 Jumbo Jet.

1974
Boeing introduces the world's most successful modern fighter, the F-15 Eagle.

1994
Boeing develops the 777 airliner.

Boeing returns $475 million in overcharges to the U.S. government.

1995
The C-17 transporter enters service, setting 22 world records during testing.

A 69-day strike costs Boeing $2 billion.

1996
Boeing buys Rockwell International's defense and space units.

DarkStar flies for the first time.

1997
Boeing merges with McDonnell Douglas to become the world's largest aerospace company.

1998
Boeing lays off 48,000 employees.

Glossary

aerospace All the companies that create technology and products to enable travel in the Earth's atmosphere and into space.

aviation The operation of aircraft.

ballistic missile A missile that is guided only at the time of launch and then falls freely to its target. By contrast, guided missiles are powered and steered throughout their time in the air.

bankruptcy When a company (or individual) cannot pay its debts, it may be forced to go out of business. It then pays creditors with any money that is left. This process is called bankruptcy.

civilian Referring to a country's citizens, as opposed to its military.

cruise missile Guided missiles that fly low, using radar to avoid hitting anything on the way to their target.

diversify To increase the variety of products a company sells or produces.

fuselage The central body of an aircraft where the crew, passengers, and cargo travel.

Global Positioning System (GPS) Satellites that transmit signals to earth. When signals from these satellites are received, they can pinpoint a person or object's location.

inventory The list of products produced by a company or products that it currently has in stock.

jet An airplane with an engine that mixes compressed air with fuel to force hot air through the engine, pushing the airplane forward at great speed.

lay off To dismiss employees not because they are doing a poor job but because the company needs to save money.

merger The combining of two or more companies into a single larger company.

metal fatigue	When metal breaks apart from repeated stress.
missiles	Rockets with explosive weapons used to destroy a target from a distance.
monopolies	The ownership and control of a product or an industry by single companies.
navigation	The science of directing a ship, aircraft, or spacecraft from one place to another.
radar	A device that detects radio waves to determine the location, distance and speed of an object.
rocket boosters	Rockets that help launch another craft, such as the space shuttle or a missile.
rotors	Large, rotating propellers attached to the top of a helicopter that enable it to fly.
seaplanes	Airplanes with floats instead of wheels so they can take off and land on water.
stealth	The design of an aircraft that avoids vertical surfaces and uses special paint so that radar signals are absorbed, making the plane difficult for an enemy to spot.
stratosphere	The upper portion of the atmosphere, which extends from approximately seven miles (11 kilometers) to about 31 miles (50 kilometers) above the Earth. Temperature changes little in the stratosphere, and clouds are rare.
strike	To stop working in an attempt to force an employer to agree to certain demands, such as an increase in pay or fewer layoffs.
tactical missile	A missile with a short range for use at the battlefront.

Index

Air Commerce Act, 8
Air Force One, 25
airplanes, ability to fly of, 12-13
Apollo spaceship, 31
aviation
    and civilian travel, 8
    and crashes, 22
    and first flight, 4
    and first transatlantic flight, 23
    history of, 4-5
    and the military, 5, 7
AWACS, 28

B & W Company, 5
    first plane produced by, 5, **8**
bankruptcy, 17
Bell Helicopters, 29
Bernoulll, Daniel, 13
Bernoulli effect, the, 13
Boeing, Bill, **6**
    and aircraft company, founding of, 5, 38
    first flight of, 4-5
    and lumber business, 6, 7
    retirement of, 11, 14
Boeing Air Transport Company, 8-9
Boeing Company
    business units of, 19
    and civilian airplanes, 9, 11, 15-16, 20,
        22-23, 36, 38
    employees of, 7, **17,** 19, 21, 36, 38
    and energy, 38-39
    and factories of, **9,** 36
        camouflage of, 18-19
        world's largest, 23
    financial problems of, 7, 17, 38
    first plane produced by, 5, **8,** 41
    and helicopters, 28-29, 36
    and lay offs, 7, 19, 21, 38
    and mail delivery, 8-9
    and military aircraft, 5, 7-8, 11, 15, 17-20,
        26-29, 36
    and missiles, 30-31
    and pressurized cabin, **16**

and profits, 10, 21, 38
and rocket boosters, 31
and satellites, 32-36
and seaplanes, 7
and spacecraft, 31-32
and strike, 38
and U.S. government, overcharging of, 37
bombers
    B-1, 26
    B-2 stealth, 26, **29**
    B-17 (Flying Fortress), 15, 19
    B-29 Superfortress, **18,** 19
    B-47, 20, 21
    B-52 Superfortress , **20,** 21
British Aerospace, 27

Eads, Jane, 9

civilian aircraft
    Comet, the, 22
    DC-2, the, 15
    Electra, the, 15
    model 40, the, 9-10, **10**
    model 247, the, 11, **11,** 15
    model 314 (Clipper), the, 15, 25
    model 707 (Dash 80), the, 22-23, **22,** 23, 25, 28
    model 737, the, 23
    model 747, the, **12, 13,** 21, 23, **24,** 25, **25,** 41
    model 767, the, 27
    model 777, the, 23
Cold War, the 20

DarkStar, 36, **37, 40**
De Havilland, 22
Delta launch vehicle, 35
diversify, 21, 36
Douglas, 15
drag, 12-13
Dyna-Soar, 31

fighter jets
    F-15 Eagle, 27
    F-22 Raptor, 27

fuel tankers/transporters
   C-17, 27, **28**
   KC-10, 27
   KC-135A, 27
fuselage, 11
Future X Pathfinder, 38

General Motors, 32
gravity, 12-13
Great Depression, the, 14
Gulf War, 27

Hamilton Steel, 15
Harrier jump jet, 27
helicopters
   CH-47 Chinook, 29
   H-46 Sea Knight, 28-29
   RAH-66 Comanche, 29
   V-22 Osprey, 29
Highly Reusable Space Transportation, 32

jet technology, 20
Jumbo Jet, 21, 23

lift, 12-13
Lockheed, 15
Lockheed Martin, 37
Lunar Orbital Vehicles, 31
Lunar Rover Vehicles, 32

McDonnell Douglas
   and merger with Boeing, 23
metal fatigue, 22
missiles, 21, 30-31
   Bomarc, 30
   Minuteman, 30
monopolies, 14-15

NASA, 31, 38
National Missile Defense (NMD), 31
navigation, 32

Newton, Isaac, 12-13
Northrop-Grumman, 29

Pan-Am, 22-23
Pratt & Whitney, 9, 15
   and Boeing merger, 10

radar, 26
Rockwell International, 38
Roosevelt, Franklin D., 15, 25
rotors, 29

satellites, 32-36
   ARGOS, 34
   Global Positioning System (GPS), 32-33, **34**
Saturn S-1C, 31
Sikorsky, 29
spacecraft, 31-32
space shuttle, 32, 36
Space Station, 32, **33**, 36, 39, **39**
stealth, 26, 36
Stratocruisers, 15-17
stratosphere, 15

Teledesic Corporation, 34-35
thrust, 12-13, 23

United Aircraft and Transport (UA&T), 10-11, 15
United Airlines, 15
United Airlines Transport, 15

Vertol Aircraft Corporation, 28-29

Westervelt, Conrad, 4
World War I, 5
World War II, 15, 17-19, 30
Wright brothers, 4

Items in bold print indicate illustration.

Further Information

BOOKS:

Braybrook, Roy. *The Aircraft Encyclopedia*. NY: Simon & Schuster, 1985.

Gould, William. *Boeing*. Lincolnwood, IL: VGM Career Horizons, 1996.

Graham, Ian. *Aircraft (Built for Speed)*. Austin, TX: Raintree/Steck-Vaughn, 1998.

WEB SITES:

Visit Boeing's own Web site:
www.boeing.com

For an overview of Boeing aircraft:
www.smoky.org/%7Edlevin/boeing.html